THIS IS US

Lessons in Life and How to Live

Bluestreak
BOOKS

Bluestreak
BOOKS

Weldon Owen International
1045 Sansome Street
San Francisco, CA 94111
www.weldonowen.com

ISBN 978-1-68188-473-8
10 9 8 7 6 5 4 3 2 1
2022 2021 2020 2019
Printed in China

Contents

We're their parents. We do the best we can. But at the end of the day—what happens to them, how they turn out—that's bigger than us.

Jack

Introduction

The Pearson family's story begins with the birth of the Big Three—three babies brought together by genetics, serendipity, and perhaps a bit of magic. From the moment they're born, these three human beings become the heart of a family that extends and expands in ways that are sometimes painful, and other times joyous—but always surprising.

Over the years, Randall, Kate, and Kevin are guided by their parents, Jack and Rebecca; their partners; and their friends. They in turn guide others through the ups and downs—the lemons and the lemonade—of lives well lived.

Together, the family faces love, loss, big decisions, and big disappointments. They mourn together, heal together, and learn together. This book gathers the best of these moments—in images and quotations—and shares their lessons for life.

Jack, your back was built to carry your son through life. Are you willing to hold him up, no matter what comes his way?

Ray (dojo)

1 Showing Up

Sometimes you just need to show up. This is a lesson the Pearson family lives by. Whether it's William and Randall creating a biological father–son relationship in the final months of William's life, the entire family supporting Kevin through his recovery, Randall being at Kate's side during her IVF surgery, or Kevin sacrificing his career dreams to be there when Randall has a breakdown.

The Pearsons may not be a perfect family—but they always manage to be there for one another during the times when it matters most.

When I was a little boy, I didn't know what I wanted to be when I grew up. Adults always ask little kids that . . . I never had a good answer. Not until I was twenty-eight. Till the day that I met you. That's when I knew exactly what I wanted to be when I grew up: I wanted to be the man that made you happy.

Jack

Randall: I got to take a client out.

Beth: Tonight? No way.

Randall: No, Beth, you don't understand. This guy Sanjay is kicking my ass.

Beth: Yeah, and so is taking care of your father and our two freaked-out daughters. No. I call marriage tonight. I'm sorry, baby. I need my teammate.

Miguel: The thing is, your wife is the gold standard of wives. She's smart, funny, beautiful, great personality, greater ass . . .

Jack: Easy.

Miguel: She's raising not one, not two, but three eight-year-olds while you sit here drinking not one, not two, but soon to be three bourbons by 5:05 p.m.

Jack: I know all this, Miguel.

Miguel: Yeah? Because as your loyal best friend, it is my duty to remind you of what you've got there. You married way, way above your station. I'd be careful not to give her a reason to notice.

I keep thinking about my wife and how I just want to get home to her, hang out with her, make sure she's okay. Which is crazy, because she's at her absolute worst right now. I mean, *Exorcist*-level bad. But I still don't want to escape her. I want to freeze time with them

I was trying to remember myself tonight, Jack. The person I used to be. And I'm not the only one who gave up on my dreams. We both did, right? And we realized an even bigger dream, an even more massive dream. When I watch Tom Hanks, I sit there and I think to myself, "He's not so great." And who does that? Who watches Tom Hanks and thinks, "You know what? I'm married to a man that's better than that."

Rebecca

You know, my life before I met you . . . it wasn't great. I just tried to get away. Get away from my neighborhood. Get away from my father. Just get away from everything. But now they say that if I want to fix myself, I've got to sit in that. I've got to sit in all the ugly, horrible years. And they say that on the other side of it, there's relief.

Jack

I came here today because last year, when I was at my lowest . . . I was crying on the floor and I was shaking. You were there for me, man. And I wanted to be there for you today and I wasn't. I did a bad job today and I'm sorry.

Randall

This is the scariest part. Some people think the scariest part is coming to the hospital to have the baby. Nah. The scariest part is leaving the hospital with the baby.

Doctor K.

I'm trying, okay? Look, I know that I'm bigger than you. I know that I'm an adult, but . . . this is my first time, too. I got three of you and I'm trying. And I'm gonna be there, okay?

Jack

Kevin: Do you remember what you wore the first day of fourth grade?

Sophie: No, of course not.

Kevin: Overalls. You had on overalls, and you had one of those scrunchie things in your hair, and you had a Punky Brewster backpack. You were walking into my fourth-grade class . . . That's the best thing that ever happened to me in my entire life. Actually, scratch that, that's not true. It's the second-best thing that ever happened to me. The best thing that ever happened to me was you telling me that you'd marry me. I'm still in love with you. And I will be at our restaurant bright and early tomorrow. I'll be sitting in our booth, waiting for you.

Rebecca: If you hurt him . . .

William: I won't.

Rebecca: Fine, then. But know this: my son, who I raised, is gonna put everything he has into trying to save you, because that's who he is. It's gonna come in front of his job, in front of his marriage, and in front of his time with his kids. So you better damn well be worth that.

I knew if I told you I was leaving, you'd try and stop me like you are right now. You'd try and stop me 'cause you were raised to be a good man. But I wasn't the one who raised you that way, Randall. I just can't step in forty years later and enjoy the fruits of someone else's labor.

William

I wound up on this side of the glass. And you wound up over there, no doubt 'cause things broke your way. Don't you dare say I'm in here by choice. People who have choices say that mess. Deja's the one good thing I've done, and I thank you for watching out for her, but make no mistake: You can give her your money, and you can give her your cheerleading, but I gave her my blood. And if you want to know what's best for her, it's me. And the second I get out of here, I'm coming back for her.

Shauna

Kate, I am here to take the first steps in overcoming our insanity one last time, for both of us. Because it's Christmas. And because we're good together. I'm back on the diet. Not for you, for me. But also for you so that you'll be with me. I can live without pizza and cookies and potato chips and . . . whatever that brownie thing was that they were serving on the plane. The one thing I cannot live without . . . is you.

Toby

The truth is I'm strong. And the things that I've been through have made me tough as hell. So if you think this is gonna scare me away, you've got another thing coming. I'm gonna get you through this, Tobe. And if you fall again, I will be right here to pick you back up. In sickness and health, for better, for worse. I'm talking forever.

Kate

He pushed a stranger on me. And that stranger became my child. And that child became my life.

Rebecca

2 Making Decisions

The Big Three all started with a big decision, a rash decision, a decision that changed the Pearson family's life. When Jack and Rebecca adopted Randall, an abandoned infant born the same day as their children Kate and Kevin, they completed their family.

This legacy of Pearson decision-making continues to shape their lives in good and bad ways—from Kate's decision to undergo IVF, to Randall's decision to abandon his career for a more fulfilling dream, to Rebecca's decision to keep Randall's biological father from him. Through it all, the decisions made and yet to be made loom large in the life of the Pearson family.

You are Jack Pearson's son. You have inside of you. And when you're nerv you're at your most nerve-racking m the curtain's about to go up . . . all y have to do is remind yourself of tha about what he'd do . . . and you'll b

Miguel

Kate: Kevin, I've known you your whole life. Well, except for those two minutes at the beginning. You've succeeded at everything you've ever tried. So here's what's gonna happen. You're gonna go to that party, and you're gonna march up to that network guy, and you're gonna tell him, "Manny out!"

Kevin: Manny out? Manny out! Let me ask you a question . . . What did I ever do those first two minutes without you?

Kate: Oh, you cried, and you crapped a lot.

Sometimes in marriage, someone has to be the one to push to make the big moves.

Rebecca

I was so sure that being skinny would make me happy. My whole life, I had that voice in my head just screaming, just shouting at me, "Lose the weight. Try harder. You're fat, and you're pathetic." And so I did it. I lost the weight. But listening to that voice my whole life, I didn't know who I was without it. I was more comfortable being fat, because I actually liked being mad at myself all the time.

Toby: Well, no more background singing for you. Your voice is way too beautiful to only be heard in a bathroom. Today is your day, babe. We are on our way to your first big gig.

Kate: Toby, there is no way in hell that I'm gonna sing in front of people.

Toby: Well, then you'll be depriving the world.

Kate: Well, the world will live.

Toby: Yes, but your audience may not. I booked you in their prime slot, three p.m. It's right after Jell-O but before their nap. Now, remember, most of 'em will probably be asleep. The rest won't remember this tomorrow. And most of them lived through World War II, so no matter how bad you are, they've seen worse.

Because I grew up in a white house, you think I don't live in a black man's world? The one where that salesman there has been eyeballing us ever since we came in here? Or where that security guard has moved just a little off his mark so he can keep us in his sight? Plus, a million things every day that I have to *choose* to let go, just so I'm not pissed off all the time. Like I have done every day of my life. Now, try on the damn slim-cut flat-front chinos. I think they'll look nice on you.

Randall

I know you're searching for something. Nobody supports your searches more than I do, baby, but recently it feels like you are somewhere in outer space. I need you to go back to work. It's not about money. I think it'll be good for you. For us. Can you do that? Can you come down from outer space and be in the real world with me?

Annie: How come Mommy goes to work now, and you stay home and are the girl?

Randall: Annie, it is incredibly old-fashioned and upsetting that you just said that. It is perfectly normal for a mommy to go to work and a daddy to stay at home. Women can do anything. Look at Hillary Clinton.

Tess: She lost.

Randall: Yeah, but she almost won. Just eat your breakfast.

You have two brothers who know exactly what they want to do with their life. But you aren't your brothers. You don't know what your path is just yet, and you know what? I think that's okay. Keep your options open. You go to some incredible liberal arts college, and you can study a bunch of different subjects until you figure out what you're passionate about.

Rebecca

WOODSIDE CAREER DAY

There's this whole genetic side of me that nobody even knew existed. William was a poet, an artist, a musician. Maybe I've had an artistic side in me all along and nobody knew to empower it.

Randall

Beth: When I was young, all I did was dream of living alone. Like some hippie life, you know? Like in some artist loft downtown. No husband. Definitely no kids.

William: So what happened?

Beth: I met your damn son . . . One look in his eyes, he ruined everything.

Rebecca: How can I leave them, Jack? Kevin's having sex, Randall's giving himself stress ulcers, Kate is—I don't even know what Kate's doing, but she's wearing a ton of eyeliner, so that can't be good. I can't go. I got to call the band, and tell them I'm not going.

Jack: No, no. You're going.

Your mom and me, we always try to treat you kids the same. Hasn't always worked because, well, you're not all the same. You're adopted and we don't talk about that enough, because to me you are every part my son. Maybe I don't want you to feel like you stand out, but I need you to know something. I *want* you to stand out. I love you as much as a human heart can, kiddo. So don't let your dad's poor choices make you feel afraid to be different.

Jack

Deja: You know what Randall told me one time? He called me exceptional. And he said it so easy, like it wasn't a big deal. I remember thinking, *he must think people have told me this before*. I bet he's told you before that you're exceptional, because you are.

Beth: Oh, but I don't know that . . .

Deja: Randall thinks so. He loves you like he's in a Disney movie or something, like he hears tiny forest animals singing or playing kazoos or something whenever you walk into a room. But if you're sad, then you should talk to him. He'll tell you you're exceptional, and he'll say it so easy that you'll believe it.

Jack: We're great together, and I love our life. But the older we get, the more I think that there's got to be something bigger than just me and you.

Rebecca: Well, thank you very much for involving me in this huge invisible change of yours. *Huge*. Because you knew when you met me and married me that I did not want to be one of those women whose sole purpose in life was to be a mother. If that's what you wanted, you should have married my mom.

Jack: I was thinking more your sister.

Close your eyes. I want you to picture the love of your life. Imagine that you have thirty seconds to win her back. One shot, three sentences. What are those sentences, and who are you saying them to? There it is.

Toby

Do you remember what Dad used to say? When something crappy would happen to us? Whenever we'd get down, whenever we felt like life wasn't going our way? "There's no lemon so sour that you can't make something resembling lemonade."

Kate

3 ## Losing

The Pearson family's journey begins with the devastating loss of a newborn child. The same day, Rebecca and Jack open their hearts to another child born that day. The Big Three are born. When Jack dies suddenly and the Big Three are only seventeen years old, it is the resilience their father taught them that helps Randall, Kate, and Kevin move on. And when Kate suffers a miscarriage and Randall must again lose a father, Jack's— and Doctor K.'s—words echo: they make something resembling lemonade.

Doctor K.: She lost a baby, Jack. You can't just dismiss that.

Jack: So did I.

Doctor K.: And you took your grief and you channeled it into action. You willed yourself forward with positivity, but Rebecca's gonna have to do this in her own way, and you're just gonna have to give her the space to do it.

Jack: What if she doesn't find her way?

Doctor K.: She will.

Jack: How do you know?

Doctor K.: For the same reason that I know you're gonna give her the space to find it. 'Cause I believe in good people. Of course, I voted for Nixon, so you got to take everything I say with a grain of salt.

For as long as I can remember, I've woken up at 6:30 every day to make Shelly coffee—splash of milk, two sugars. I would make it and bring it to her in bed. And then one day, woke up, 6:30 . . . like always, and I made myself one. I just didn't feel like making Shelly one. And the worst part is . . . she didn't even notice. We stopped noticing each other. We stopped trying to make each other happy. When we realized that, we knew it was over. Now, I think that every single couple has a handful of these moments when you reach a crossroads. They're make-or-break, these moments. And you either roll up your sleeves and you fight for what you've got or you decide that you're tired . . . and you give up. And I had one of these moments . . . when I didn't make Shelly her coffee.

Miguel

Beth: Honey, you can't be playing chess at three in the morning.

Tess: But Grandpa's always napping when I get home from school. And I have soccer on Saturdays. You said he's not going to be around forever, so I have to play with him as much as I can now.

It seems your grandpa left you some instructions. "Dear Tess and Annie, I know you're probably feeling a little sad right now, and I'd like to get you back to smiling. Because you have two of my all-time favorite smiles. That's why I'd like you two to plan my memorial. Adults make these things sad, and I want you two to make it fun. Fill it with

Kevin: What happened is my dad died. And I hated him for it. And I couldn't eat for a month, and I used to wake myself up crying so I could cry myself back to sleep again.

Olivia: Why do you push all of that away? You can't just kill the feelings like they're some creature that you're afraid of. That pain is a part of you; I can see it now. I can feel it.

Doctor K.: You are the same woman who lost a child, and rolled out of my hospital with three babies just the same. You're as tough as they come, Rebecca Pearson.

Rebecca: Not without him.

Doctor K.: Bull crap.

Kate: How can I be this sad? I never even met the baby. I never held him. Or her. It wasn't even old enough for me to know.

Rebecca: I never held Kyle. I remember they asked me if I wanted to, because it helps mothers with closure. To hold the baby and to say goodbye. But I didn't want to do that because I felt like if I didn't hold him, somehow it would lessen the pain, which wasn't the case, obviously, because I knew him already. And then the wondering set in. *Did I do this? Did I do something wrong? Did I sleep on the wrong side? Should I have gone on that walk?* 'Cause the day you guys were born, I went on this long, hot walk.

Kate: It wasn't your fault.

Rebecca: And this wasn't yours.

Olivia: How does it feel to be dying?
William: It feels like all of these beautiful pieces of life are flying around me and I'm trying to catch them. When my granddaughter falls asleep on my lap, I try to catch the feeling of her breathing against me. And when I make my son laugh, I try to catch the sound of him laughing. How it rolls up from his chest. But the pieces are moving faster now, and I can't catch them all. I can feel them slipping through my fingertips. And soon where there used to be my granddaughter breathing and my son laughing, there will be nothing.

After your father died, I had to let go of a lot of things. And happiness was one of the first things to go, and it was like that for a very, very long time. What I found with Miguel is quieter and older. But I'm happy. He really makes me laugh.

Rebecca

Rebecca: Are you scared?

Doctor K.: Scared? Of the great beyond? Well, now, I am on quite a bit of morphine here, so that does have to be taken into account, but . . . no. I guess I would say curious. I remember the first time I walked up on the edge of the Grand Canyon. It's been pretty well talked up, so my expectations were mighty high. But still . . . it did not disappoint. Not a bit.

It's better to have loved and lost, surely. But try not to lose it at all.

William

Kevin, if you don't allow yourself to grieve Dad's death, it'll be like taking a giant breath in and just holding it there for the rest of your life.

Kate

4 Healing

Life has not always given the Pearsons an easy path, and they have not always made the right decisions. But even when the family members have become lost, they ultimately find their way home to one another. Healing—through reconciliation, honesty, and showing up—has kept the family tightly bonded no matter the obstacle. They turn to family even when—perhaps especially when—their own actions have led them astray.

Kate: It's always gonna be about the weight for me, Toby. It's been my story ever since I was a little girl. And every moment that I'm not thinking about it, I'm thinking about it. Like . . . will this chair hold me? Will this dress fit me? And if I ever get pregnant, would anyone ever notice? It's just at the core of who I am; it's just deep inside, and eight tequila shots can only mask that for a couple hours.

Toby: I know. And it was ten tequila shots, but . . . I get it. And just for the record . . . this dress is fitting you in all the right places.

What if Kate spent so much time taking care of me that she forgot to take care of herself? And year after year went by, and I should've recognized that I should've helped her.

Kevin

I was so angry, I wanted to take it out on the whole world. Instead, I took it out on Beth's mom. And on Beth. Somehow, it was my way of being loyal to my mom. Then one morning, I don't know . . . I just forgot. I forgot to hate 'em. We were all sitting at the kitchen table. And I started laughing. That was a good day. The day when it stopped making sense, hating the people who love me.

Zoe

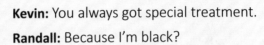

Kevin: You always got special treatment.

Randall: Because I'm black?

Kevin: No, because you're black and you're adopted.

Randall: Oh, yeah, hit the jackpot with that combination. Couldn't have had it any easier.

Kevin: In our house, you did. With our mother, you did.

You know, for a minute there, you actually convinced me that I was like you. That deep down, I was just damaged goods. And then I realized, that's ridiculous. Do I have issues? Yes. But deep down, I'm awesome.

Kate

You're not ready. But one day, I know you're going to sit back down at this piano and start singing again. Because it's gonna be a place where you can put all of that sadness. And because it's what you're meant to do.

Rebecca

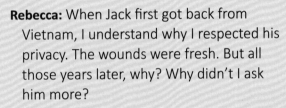

Rebecca: When Jack first got back from Vietnam, I understand why I respected his privacy. The wounds were fresh. But all those years later, why? Why didn't I ask him more?

Miguel: You know, Jack was my closest friend, for over twenty years, but I didn't know him completely. Not the stuff from before. I think that there was a darkness inside of him. I think that he was afraid. You know, if that darkness got out, then it might swallow up the light that he got from you. From the kids. And make no mistake: you and the kids were everything.

My mom was skinny and gorgeous. Well, *is* gorgeous. She still gets hit on by everyone. She once was asked if she was a model when she had the flu. Pretty hard growing up with a mom like that. I'd spend all my time comparing myself to her and then I took it out on her, and now we barely talk and it sucks. See, your mom is not perfect. She has her stuff and you have yours, but you've got to cut her a break or you are going to regret it, I promise.

Kate

Hey, Dad. I haven't been here since the funeral. Usually I try to avoid you today, which is ironic, 'cause I could really use you about right now. So I figured what the heck, I would just come here and try to just . . . say some of the things that I never got a chance to. I have had a really bad year. I had a bad couple of decades, actually. I just think you'd be really disappointed in me. I'm just . . . . really struggling. I wanted to stop avoiding you, and I wanted to just talk to you. And tell you that I'm sorry . . . and tell you that I'm gonna do better. And if it's the last thing I do, I'm gonna make you proud of me. It might take me another couple of decades to get there, but I will get there. You got to bear with me, though, okay?

Kevin

You're scared that you'll lose all the weight, and that nothing will have changed, right? That you will discover that the person who you've always been is who you truly are. And all your dreams of the kind of life you're gonna lead one day are nothing more than lies you've told yourself.

And for twenty years, I thought very little of myself. And then this big old guy with this big old heart came walking into my support group. And then, when I would break, he never gave up on me, over and over again, never gave up on me and made me believe in me. Do you know that you changed my life, that you saved my life?

Kate

Jesse: I was invited to my sister's house. But the people there will ask me how I'm doing, and I'm in no mood to spin lies about the joys of being sober.

William: You stay sober, you won't have to lie about it. Look, tonight a bunch of us sober musicians are getting together. On the holidays we like to play, mostly to keep us from getting into trouble. You're welcome to come.

Jesse: Good Lord. Listening to jazz sober sounds awful.

Yeah, and you remind me of him, you know that? The way that you move your hands when you talk. The way you walk across a room. Sometimes you remind me of him so much that the hair on my arm stands up. It's why it breaks my heart that you don't like me, Kevin. Because when I'm around you, I feel like I get a little piece of my best friend back.

Miguel

Mom, I know that our stuff . . . it can be complicated sometimes. But it's because all that I've ever wanted was to be like you. Mom, you are not *in* my way. You *are* my way.

Kate

I fall a little bit more in love with you every day. In you, I have found my soul mate, my best friend, my lover, my partner, my safe place. You are my great love story. And Jack Pearson . . . our story is just getting started.

Rebecca

5 Loving

I t was a love story that started it all. When Jack and Rebecca fell for each other, they could have never known how far and wide their love would spread.

Their love inspires the Big Three throughout their lives—in their relationships with each other, with their partners, and with their own children. It allows Randall to be the father who would do anything for his wife and children and also allows him to open his heart to William and Deja. Jack's love helps heal Rebecca's grief for her child—and allows her to find new love after Jack's death. Her parents' love allows Kate to invest everything in her relationship with Toby, and perhaps even risk her own life to have a child; and it's this love that inspires Kevin to keep looking for his own happy ending even after so many stumbles.

For the twenty-two years that I worked at Lundy Builders, my wife put a folded note packed into my briefcase every day. The highlight of my day in the office was opening one of those little scraps of paper. Now, when Rebecca and I started Big Three Homes, she stopped writing the lunch notes. But I was okay with that. I had the highlight of my day sitting right there by my side. Every day.

Jack

Kate: You're the only good thing in my life, Kev.

Kevin: I'm not that great.

Kate: I know. That's what makes it worse.

We're twins. We're not like regular people. When I was a kid, I broke my arm and he cried out in pain ten miles away. We're that connected.

Kate

I am thankful for my family. I'm thankful that we're all safe. And there's no one in the world I'd rather be too hot or too cold with.

Jack

You never knew my dad Jack. But oh, man, he was the best dad ever. All I ever wanted to do with my life was be half the dad he was. And I was so scared about that. That I wouldn't be good when the time came. And then you were born. And my life flipped. It did a somersault. And I realized I don't even have to try at this. I'm gonna be the best dad ever because I love this little girl so much that I don't even have a choice. You're my number one, baby girl. You're the little girl who made my life somersault.

Randall

I used to watch romantic comedies where the perfect, charming Hugh Grant guy would bend over backwards for the woman that he loves. And I would think, "If I could have that, then I would be happy." And then I met you, and you were better than them. You were better than my wildest dreams.

Kate

Katie-girl, Tobias. When I look at you, I know in my bones that in choosing each other, you have chosen perfectly.

Randall

Don't stop trying to make me see myself the way you see me.

Kate

Kate: I don't really know who I am if I'm not your sister.

Kevin: I do. You're gonna love her.

You know, Beth, we've been together for seventeen years. I know your face, your hands, your soul better than I know my own. You don't have to censor yourself. Ever. Not with me.

Randall

Randall: My mother said there's no such thing as a perfect marriage. But on that, I have to disagree with my mother.

Beth: I didn't think that was allowed.

Randall: Today I'm allowing it. Because we're perfect, Beth. And I know this because I'm a perfectionist. And I fail and I fail . . . and the failure leads to self-doubt and self-loathing, and it's all this other crap I got muddled up inside here. But when it comes to you and me . . . Baby, there ain't nothing muddled there. We are perfect together. We are perfectly imperfect. You see, we don't follow one another, Beth. We don't push our own plans on each other. We adjust our plans together. And if I can't adjust to you, then . . . I have to figure out another way to do this.

I love the mother that you are. I love that you are still the most beautiful woman in any room and that you laugh with your entire face. I love that you dance funny and not sexy, which makes it even sexier. But most of all, I love that you are still the same woman who, all those years ago, ran out of a blind date because she simply had to sing. You're not just my great love story, Rebecca. You were my big break.

Jack

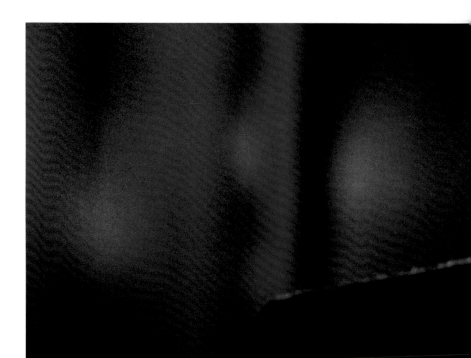

The baby didn't come from this. It came from love. His mother? . . . We met on that bus, actually. My world spun on every axis that day. I read poetry to her the first time we talked.

William

Baby, one day, I'm gonna buy you the best washing machine in the world.

Jack

You're gonna find your balance, Randall. And then you're gonna lose it, and then you're gonna find it again. That's the ride. And you're gonna make a lot of choices, and I'm probably not gonna be around for all of them. The choices you make are gonna be spectacular, because you are spectacular, Son.

Jack

6 Living

I f there is one thing the Pearsons know, it's that life is messy and unpredictable. As much as you try to plan for it, it will always throw you curveballs. It's how you handle those curveballs that makes the difference.

Jack Pearson always had the perfect line to sum up life's ups and downs, and he and Rebecca taught the Big Three how to adapt to them. From Kevin's decision that uncertainty was better than being the Manny, to Kate's realization that her life was bigger than being Kevin's twin sister, to Randall's acceptance that he can't control every outcome, it is always Jack's voice whispering in their ear.

William: Roll all your windows down, Randall. Crank up the music. Grow out that 'fro. Let someone else make your bed.

Randall: I like making my damn bed, old man.

My father once told me that I was gonna be a great man. And my whole life, in the back of my mind, I always wanted to be one. I'm starting to think it might be harder to be a good man than a great one.

Randall

I'm sorry, Kate. I'm an idiot. I . . . don't think you're sad and damaged. I don't know why I said that. The truth is, I am insanely proud of you and everything you've accomplished over the past year, the weight loss, and the therapy. Meeting a guy who can burp the alphabet.

Kevin

Kate: I know you have a mom, but if there's anything you ever want to talk to me about, anytime. I mean, pretty soon you're gonna have your first kiss, and your first boyfriend.

Tess: Or girlfriend.

Kate: Or girlfriend. Yeah, or . . . girlfriend.

Deja: So, who's in charge here? Your mom and dad . . . who makes all the rules?

Tess: They both do, but . . .

Tess and Annie: Mom.

You find your soul mate, you get married, you stay together until you die, period.

Jack

Sometimes a baby dies right in the beginning. But your dad and I had all this room in our hearts for three babies. And we saw you. We met you. So you are a miracle. But you're not "instead" of anything. You're the way it was always supposed to be.

Rebecca

Look, we have had three lunches and four dinner dates. We have made out seven times and heavy-petted twice. Our plane is rapidly approaching the boyfriend-girlfriend zone, and I, for one, am preparing myself for landing. But I need to know that everything isn't gonna always be about our weight. All right? We need to be able to cut loose at parties. We need to get really dressed up. We need to have sex. I just slipped that in there very casually because I think that's something that we should start doing very soon.

Toby

And if life breaks for you the way it would not break for me, if love hunts you, finds you, captures you, will you hold it tight, nurture it, protect it?

William

The sexiest thing about you is how sexy you
make me feel.

Kate

No. You will not dismiss me like that. And you will not dismiss me because I don't look like that girl up there. I know I'm not what you imagined, but I will not walk out of this room and allow you to just give this gig to a lesser singer because she's a size 2. Because I've been living versions of that story my entire life, and I can't do it anymore. And I won't do it anymore.

Kate

When you first told me what you did
for a living—man, I didn't understand
a word, hand to God. You might as well
have been speaking German. But I was
watching your face. In my better days, I've
met and played with some of the greatest
musicians in the world. And when they
talked about music, their face looked
like your face when you told me about
whatever the hell it is you do.

Beth: Miguel says it's because you feel like you need to be the rock for them, and apologizing shows vulnerability.

Randall: I'm sorry, uh, Miguel's weighing in on this now?

Beth: Me, him, and Toby have a text chain. It's mostly GIFs, but, you know, sometimes we talk about how messed up y'all are.

Rebecca: I know. Take the sourest lemons and make something resembling lemonade, right?

Doctor K.: You didn't just make something resembling lemonade, dear. You made one of the sweetest damn pitchers of lemonade I ever saw.

I painted this because I felt like the play was about life. And life is full of color. And we each get to come along and we add our own color to the painting. And even though it's not very big—the painting—you sort of have to figure that it goes on forever . . . in each direction . . . And it's really crazy if you think about it—isn't it?—that a hundred years ago, some guy that I never met came to this country with a suitcase. He has a son, who has a son, who has me. At first, when I was painting, I was thinking . . . maybe up here, that was that guy's part of the painting and then . . . down here, that's my part of the painting. And then I started to think, well, what if . . . we're all in the painting, everywhere?

And what if we're in the painting before we're born? What if we're in it after we die? And these colors that we keep adding, what if they just keep getting added on top of one another, until eventually we're not even different colors anymore? We're just . . . one thing. One painting.

It all just sort of fits somehow. And even if you don't understand how yet, people will die in our lives, people that we love. In the future. Maybe tomorrow. Maybe years from now. I mean, it's kind of beautiful—the fact that just because someone dies, just because you can't see them or talk to them anymore, it doesn't mean they're not still in the painting. I think maybe that's the point of the whole thing. There's no dying. There's no you or me or them. It's just us. And this sloppy, wild, colorful, magical thing that has no beginning, it has no end . . . this right here . . . I think it's us.

Kevin